COCONUT
The Tree of Life

By Carolyn Meyer

Milk, Butter, and Cheese

Saw, Hammer, and Paint,
Woodworking and Finishing for Beginners

By Carolyn Meyer with Jerome Wexler

Rock Tumbling,
From Stones to Gems to Jewelry

COCONUT
The Tree of Life

CAROLYN MEYER

illustrated by Lynne Cherry

William Morrow and Company
New York 1976

Printed in the United States of America.

1   2   3   4   5   6   7   8   9   10

Library of Congress Cataloging in Publication Data

Meyer, Carolyn.
    Coconut, the tree of life.

    SUMMARY: Discusses the growth, cultivation, processing, and uses of coconuts. Includes thirty coconut recipes.
    1. Coconut palm—Juvenile literature.   2. Coconut—Juvenile literature.
3. Cookery (Coconut)—Juvenile literature.   [1. Coconut palm.   2. Coconut.
3. Cookery—Coconut]   I. Cherry, Lynne.   II. Title.
SB401.C6M48   641.3′4′61   76-22673
ISBN 0-688-22084-3
ISBN 0-688-32084-8

The author wishes to thank Mr. Andrew M. Hay of Calvert, Vavasseur & Company, Inc. for his kind assistance and advice in preparation of this book.

Contents

A Luxurious Necessity

What is the most useful tree in the world?

Unless you live in certain parts of the tropics, that question could keep you guessing for a long time. The answer comes as a surprise to people in North America; it's the coconut palm.

Coconuts are oddities in many supermarkets in the United States—big, hairy-looking brown nuts with three dark spots on one end that form what looks a little like a monkey face. It is difficult to crack open a coconut, unless you know how, and hard to pry the white meat away from the shell. Usually it seems much easier to pick a package of shredded coconut off the shelf and forget about the nut.

For most Americans, coconut is a luxury. Its snow-white meat adds a glamorous touch to a cake or a pie and extra crunch in a cookie, but in such small quantities it does not contribute much extra food value to our diet. One reason the coconut has luxury status is because very few grow on this continent. The graceful coconut palms in the southern part of Florida are grown primarily for landscape decoration, not for food or other uses.

But on the other side of the world in the Philippines, there is a saying, "He who plants a coconut tree plants vessels and clothing, food and drink, a habitation for himself, and a heritage for his children." In the Philippines, and in many other parts of the world, the coconut is the backbone of the economy and a basic part of the diet. The coconut palm, picturesque symbol of tropical lands, is called the "tree of life" by the people who live there.

Every part of the coconut palm has its uses. There is, of course, the white meat of the nut, which is used for food. The meat is also the source of coconut oil, which is used for cooking and has a number of nonfood uses too, making it of great importance in world trade. In addition, the shell of the coconut and the husk, the roots of the tree, its fronds and flowers, and the wood of the trunk itself account for literally hundreds of additional uses.

Until about a century ago, coconuts were not much known outside of the tropics. When they were brought to Europe and America by seamen and travelers, they were regarded as curiosities. But as they became more plentiful, cooks found ways to use them. One of the earliest ways of eating coconut in this country was in a dessert called "ambrosia." According to Greek and Roman mythology, ambrosia was the food eaten by the gods to preserve their immortality. But in the American South, it was a combination of coconuts and oranges. Columbus had first brought oranges to the West Indies, and orange trees soon flourished in what is now Florida. Southern cooks arranged the two tropical luxuries in the family's best crystal bowl and served it up as the traditional finale to a sumptuous Christmas dinner.

SOUTHERN AMBROSIA

3 large, juicy oranges
3 tablespoons sugar
1 cup coconut

Peel the oranges, pull off the white fibers, and slice the oranges crosswise into thin slices. Pick out the seeds.

Arrange the slices from one orange in a pretty glass bowl. Sprinkle with 1 tablespoon of sugar and ⅓ cup of coconut. Repeat, making two more layers. Chill the ambrosia in the refrigerator for several hours before you serve it.

Serves 4.

Although few coconut palms grow in the continental United States, there are many coconuts on the islands of Hawaii, where pineapples are the leading crop. Pineapple and coconut seem to have a natural affinity for one another.

HAWAIIAN AMBROSIA

1 fresh pineapple (or one 20-ounce can of pineapple chunks)
3 tablespoons honey
1 cup coconut

If you are using a fresh pineapple, cut off the top and the rough outside. Chop the pineapple into chunks. If you are using canned pineapple, drain off the syrup.

Arrange ⅓ of the pineapple in a glass dish, drizzle 1 tablespoon of honey over it, and sprinkle with ⅓ cup of coconut. Repeat, making two more layers. Chill in the refrigerator for several hours before you serve it.

Serves 4.

You can, of course, make your own version of ambrosia with whatever fruits are in season. Bananas, apples, pears, grapes, and berries can all be used in whatever combination you like. Mix the fruits, sweeten them slightly with honey or sugar, and arrange in layers with the grated coconut. Chilling in the refrigerator helps to blend the flavors.

Ambrosia is a simple beginning. While it is no guarantee you will live forever, it is a good introduction to the many ways in which people around the world use and enjoy coconut.

Incidentally, many of these uses involve cooking, which means using knives, blenders, broilers, and other potentially dangerous tools. If you are not used to working with this equipment, ask an adult to help you or show you how to handle it safely by yourself. You'll enjoy the coconut more!

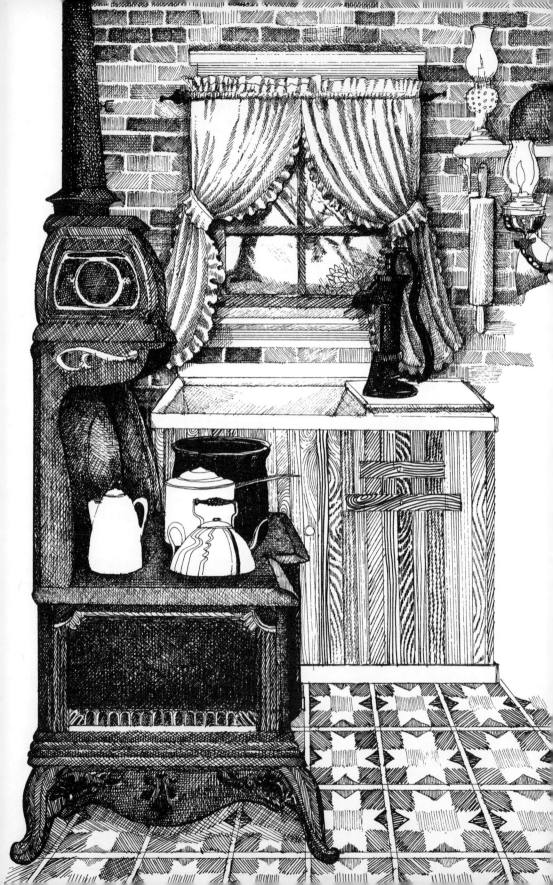

From Magellan's Voyage
to Great-Grandmother's Kitchen

In September, 1519, Ferdinand Magellan sailed from Spain with five vessels and about 265 men in search of a western route to the Spice Islands of Indonesia. Some historians believe Magellan had already reached those islands by an eastern route during an earlier, secret journey under the flag of Portugal, his own country. But he had fallen into disfavor in the Portuguese court, and he made his famous westward voyage for the Spanish.

Of all the troubles that arose on that first circumnavigation of the world, lack of food was probably the worst. Some of the ships' stores were stolen; much of what remained was spoiled. Weeks passed. Although the men spotted at least one little island clustered with coconut palms, they were forced to pass it by or run the risk of being left behind. Finally, half dead with scurvy and starvation, they reached the island of Guam.

There they were greeted by unfriendly men wearing masks of coconut shells and carrying coconut-shell rattles with human thighbones as handles. But Magellan's men were able to take on board a supply of fresh, nourishing food that included plenty of coconuts.

Aboard Magellan's ship was a Venetian nobleman, Antonio Pigafetta, who was apparently along on that extraordinary voyage as an ordinary tourist. Pigafetta kept a journal, noting in detail everything he saw. His diary became the chief source of information about the expedition. In it he described coconuts. Although earlier Sanskrit records from before 1000 B.C. made note of the coconut palm in Asia, and Marco Polo in the thirteenth century reported on the existence of the coconut in Sumatra, this was the first detailed account by a European of the peculiar tropical fruit.

"Coconuts are the fruit of the palm trees," he wrote. "And as we have bread, wine, oil, and vinegar, so they get all these things from the said trees. . . . With two of these palm trees a whole family of ten can sustain itself. . . . They last for a hundred years."

PIGAFETTA

Sir Francis Drake, who in 1577 became the first Englishman
to sail around the world, was also impressed by the coconut on
his voyage. From the Cape Verde Islands off the coast of West
Africa, he wrote, "Amongst other things we found here a kind
of fruit called Cocos, which because it is not commonly
knowen with us in England, I thought good to make some
description of it." And he did.

19

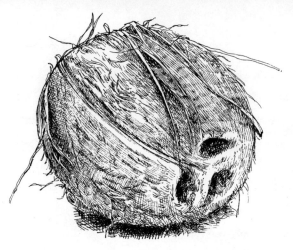

Although writers have generally agreed on the usefulness and versatility of the coconut, there has been disagreement about the spelling. *Coco* means *goblin* in Portuguese, and the odd little face formed by the three dark spots on the inner shell apparently reminded both the Portuguese and the Spanish of a goblin. But when Samuel Johnson's *Dictionary of the English Language* was published in 1755, he spelled the word *cocoanut*. This change was probably because chocolate was just coming into fashion in England, and the hot drink made from cacao beans had already been misspelled as *cocoa*. Many people, including Johnson, apparently confused the nuts with the beans and came up with *cocoanut*. Later writers dropped the *a;* some inserted a hyphen in its place.

Generations passed, but the coconut was still "not commonly knowen" anywhere but in the tropics. Then, in 1831, an Englishman named J. W. Bennett printed "A Treatise on the Coco-nut Tree, and the Many Valuable properties possessed by the Splendid Palm." These properties ranged from the medicinal use of the root to the use of charcoal from the shell for cleaning the teeth and use of coconut water by "the fair sex" as a wrinkle remover.

Within a few decades, traders in the East Indies who were importing tea and spices to Europe had also developed an interest in coconuts. Toward the end of the nineteenth century, candy making was a growing business. Techniques had been developed to produce sugar more cheaply, and people had more money to spend on little luxuries, all as a result of the Industrial Revolution. Coconut suddenly became a popular ingredient in candies and pastries.

At that time traders were shipping the whole coconut from Ceylon to London, an impractical and expensive undertaking since about half of its one-pound weight was water. Removing the shell and draining the liquid was no solution, because the exposed meat spoiled quickly in tropical temperatures. The firm of J. H. Vavasseur and Company, one of the world's first specialists in coconuts, solved the problem by desiccation: shredding the coconut meat and drying it before it was shipped. In the early 1890's, about six thousand tons a year of desiccated coconut were exported from Ceylon; within ten years that figure had been multiplied by ten. England and Europe were on a coconut kick.

Meanwhile, in the United States, coconuts arrived from the Caribbean as occasional novelties. That situation changed by the end of the nineteenth century because of a revolution. In Cuba, the guerrilla activity of patriots trying to overthrow Spanish rule was producing a shaky economy for that island. One American businessman, a flour miller in Philadelphia, found himself being paid by a Cuban debtor with a shipload

of coconuts. The businessman, Franklin Baker, was hard pressed to know what to do with all those coconuts in 1895. His first idea was to load them into freight cars and to launch a whistle-stop campaign, wiring ahead at each station to grocers and food manufacturers along the way and offering them his coconuts at very special prices.

The coconuts sold quickly, but not quickly enough. Baker still had a lot of coconuts to get rid of before they spoiled. And so he, too, set up an operation for shredding and drying the white meat, then selling the desiccated coconut to confectioners and pastry chefs. It worked. Home cooks also took a fancy to the shredded coconut, and Baker's idea proved so successful that he established a processing plant that operated for many years.

Today about 20 percent of the coconut exported from the Philippines to the United States is desiccated. The nuts are shelled by hand to protect them from damage, and the brown skin under the shell is pared away, leaving whole, white balls of coconut meat. These balls are cut open, washed, pasteurized,

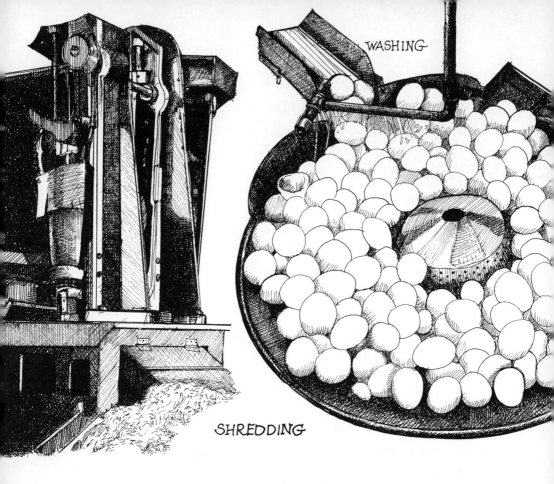

WASHING

SHREDDING

and fed into shredding machines. Depending on the way in which the coconut is to be used, it is cut into flakes and shreds of various sizes. Confectioners want one size, cookie makers another, and so forth. Consumers at large supermarket chains can usually find two choices.

The shredded coconut is dried—desiccated—in hot-air ovens. Then it is bagged and shipped in large sacks. Before it is repackaged for sale to consumers, some of the moisture that has been removed in desiccation is restored. Small amounts of sugar and propylene glycol, which prevents the growth of mold, are also added.

At the turn of the century, home cooks treated their families to an assortment of desserts that included coconut cream pie, coconut custard, coconut cookies, and coconut cakes with coconut icing, all made with desiccated coconut. The rage in those days was White Mountain Cake, a four-layer extravaganza filled and frosted with coconut icing.

Many of these old favorites are *still* favorites. Desiccated coconut is available in two general types. The shredded variety with long, wavy strands is best used for snowy, showy toppings on cakes and pies. Finely cut flaked coconut is preferable when the coconut is being combined with other ingredients. Shredded coconut can be substituted for flaked coconut if you whirl it in a blender or even snip it with scissors. Both kinds can be purchased in cans or plastic packages. Once they have been opened, keep them tightly covered to prevent drying out.

The recipes in this book do not specify which kind of coconut to use but leave the choice up to you.

OLD-FASHIONED COCONUT JUMBLES

⅔ cup butter or margarine
⅔ cup sugar
1 egg
1⅓ cup flour
1 cup coconut

Turn on the oven and let it heat to 375 degrees. Lightly grease one or two cookie sheets.

Put the sugar and butter or margarine into a mixing bowl, and blend with your hands (if the butter is cold and hard) or with a wooden spoon until they are thoroughly mixed. Add the egg and beat it in.

Add the flour and coconut and work them in, making a stiff dough. Drop by a teaspoon about 3 inches apart on the cookie sheets. Bake 10 to 12 minutes, until lightly browned. Use a spatula to lift the cookies onto a rack to cool.

Makes about 3½ dozen cookies.

A perfect coconut custard pie has always been a challenge for cooks, because piecrusts should be baked at high temperatures to keep them from getting soggy, and custards should be baked at low temperatures to keep them smooth. A simple baked custard—without the crust—is a good solution.

BAKED COCONUT CUSTARD

2 cups milk
3 eggs
⅓ cup sugar
¼ teaspoon salt
1 teaspoon vanilla
½ cup coconut

Turn on the oven and let it heat to 350 degrees.

Scald the milk by heating it slowly in a saucepan until bubbles begin to form around the sides. Don't let it boil.

While the milk is heating, break the eggs into a mixing bowl. Add the sugar and salt, and beat until the sugar is dissolved.

Add half the hot milk to the beaten eggs very slowly, stirring hard as you do to keep the eggs from cooking into lumps. Then add the rest of the milk, and stir in the vanilla and the coconut.

Pour the mixture into a 1½-quart baking dish. Set the dish in a pan that is slightly larger, and pour hot water into the pan around the baking dish until the water is about one inch deep. The water keeps the outside of the custard from cooking much faster than the center. Put the pan with the baking dish into the oven and bake for 50 minutes, or until a table knife inserted in the custard comes out clean.

Carefully take the pan out of the oven and lift out the baking dish. After the custard has cooled off, chill it in the refrigerator.

Serves 4.

A pie shell made of coconut is easy and delicious for any kind of pie that does not require baking. Make the pie shell first; then prepare the filling while the shell cools.

COCONUT PIE SHELL and TOASTED COCONUT

2 cups coconut
3 tablespoons butter or margarine

Turn on the oven and let it heat to 300 degrees.

Melt the butter or margarine in a small saucepan. Thoroughly mix the melted butter with 1½ cups of the coconut in a 9-inch pie pan. Press the mixture against the bottom and sides of the pan.

Spread the remaining ½ cup of coconut in a second pie pan.

Bake the pie shell and toast the remaining coconut for about 15 minutes. Stir the toasting coconut occasionally so that it browns evenly. Bake until both are golden brown. Let the pie shell and toasted coconut cool. Fill with coconut-cream-pie filling, or some other favorite.

COCONUT-CREAM-PIE FILLING

⅔ cup sugar
3 tablespoons cornstarch
½ teaspoon salt
3 cups milk
2 eggs
1 tablespoon butter or margarine
1½ teaspoons vanilla
½ cup coconut

Mix the sugar, cornstarch, and salt in a saucepan. Slowly add the milk, stirring it briskly, making sure there are no lumps of cornstarch left unblended.

Bring to a boil over medium heat, stirring constantly with a wooden spoon and making sure that you cover every bit of the bottom of the pan as you stir. This mixture scorches quickly if you don't. Boil gently for 1 minute and remove from the hot burner.

Beat the eggs in a small mixing bowl. Slowly pour half the milk mixture into the eggs, stirring all the time. Then pour the egg-milk mixture back into the saucepan, and stir it into the rest of the milk mixture. Bring to a boil again. Add the butter or margarine, vanilla, and coconut.

Pour the mixture into the coconut pie shell. If there is too much filling for the pie, pour the leftover into dessert dishes to serve some other time. Sprinkle the top of the pie with toasted coconut. After the pie has cooled, chill it in the refrigerator.

Serves 6.

COCONUT-OATMEAL SQUARES

½ cup brown sugar

½ cup white sugar

½ cup butter or margarine

½ teaspoon vanilla

2 eggs

1 cup flour

1 cup oatmeal

½ teaspoon salt

½ cup coconut

½ cup chopped nuts (optional)

Turn on the oven and let it heat to 375 degrees. Grease an 8-inch square baking pan or a 9-inch pie pan.

Put the two kinds of sugar and butter or margarine into a mixing bowl, and blend with your hands (if the butter is cold and hard) or with a wooden spoon until they are thoroughly mixed. Add the vanilla and eggs, and beat them in.

Stir in the flour and oatmeal, salt, coconut, and nuts, if you want them, until everything is well mixed.

Spread the mixture evenly in the pan. Bake for 30 minutes. Cool the pan on a wire rack, and then cut into coconut-oatmeal squares while still warm.

Makes 16 squares.

COCONUT-OATMEAL COOKIES

Follow the recipe for Coconut-Oatmeal Squares, *except:*

Turn on the oven to 350 degrees. Grease one or two cookie sheets.

Use only 1 egg. Mix ½ teaspoon baking soda and ½ teaspoon baking powder with the flour and oatmeal.

Drop with a teaspoon 2 inches apart on the cookie sheets. Bake 12 minutes, until lightly browned. Use a spatula to lift the cookies onto a rack to cool.

Makes about 3 dozen cookies.

COCONUT QUICKBREAD

¾ cup sugar
2 tablespoons butter or margarine
1 egg
1½ cups milk
3 cups flour
3½ teaspoons baking powder
¾ to 1 cup coconut

Turn on the oven and let it heat to 350 degrees. Grease a loaf pan, 9 by 5 by 3 inches.

Put the sugar and shortening into a mixing bowl, and blend with your hands (if the butter is cold and hard) or with a wooden spoon until they are thoroughly mixed. Add the egg and beat it in. Stir in the milk.

In a separate bowl mix the flour, baking powder, and coconut with a fork. Add these dry ingredients all at once to the sugar mixture, and stir just until everything is well mixed.

Pour the mixture into the loaf pan and spread it into the corners. Bake for 50 minutes, or until a toothpick stuck into the center of the loaf comes out clean. Tip the loaf out of the pan, loosening it around the sides with a knife, if you need to. Set it on a rack to cool completely.

Slice it thinly with a sharp knife, using a sawing motion to keep it from crumbling. Toast it, if you wish, and serve it plain or with cream cheese or fruit jam.

Makes 1 loaf.

COCONUT-ORANGE LOAF

Follow the recipe for Coconut Quickbread, *except:*
Use only ¾ cup milk and add ¾ cup orange juice and 1 tablespoon grated orange rind.

COCONUT-PINEAPPLE LOAF

Follow the recipe for Coconut Quickbread, *except:*
Use only 1 cup milk and add one 7-ounce can of crushed pineapple with its syrup.

THE FIRST GENERATION

How and Where They Grow

The coconut palm, the saying goes, is a three-generation tree. A man plants the seedling when his son is born and waits seven years until the tree begins to bear its first nuts. Another eight years pass, and the tree reaches maturity; the planter's son begins to harvest the nuts. For the next half century, the planter's son and then his grandson gather the nuts. Eventually there are fewer and fewer nuts on the old tree, until at last the grandson chops it down and replaces it with a new seedling, at the time *his* son is born. Some trees outlast all three generations.

THE SECOND
GENERATION

THE THIRD GENERATION

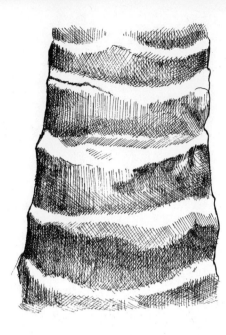

ridges on trunk

Cocos nucifera is the botanical name of the beautiful and remarkable tree that reaches a height of sixty to one hundred feet. It is branchless, a huge "stem" topped with a majestic crown of fronds. Each year the oldest fronds around the outside of the crown drop off, and new ones grow out from the center of the crown. In this way the tree becomes taller year by year, adding a new ridge where the old fronds have fallen away. There are no growth rings when the tree is cut down, but the number of ridges indicates how old the tree must be. The trunk does not become thicker, only taller, and it is of uniform thickness along all of its vast length. Its roots grip the earth deeply.

At the center of the feathery crown are flowers and nuts in all stages of ripeness, some of them tiny and green, others full-sized but still unripe. Those that have turned purplish brown have taken a full year to develop from flower bud to full ripeness and are ready to fall to the ground.

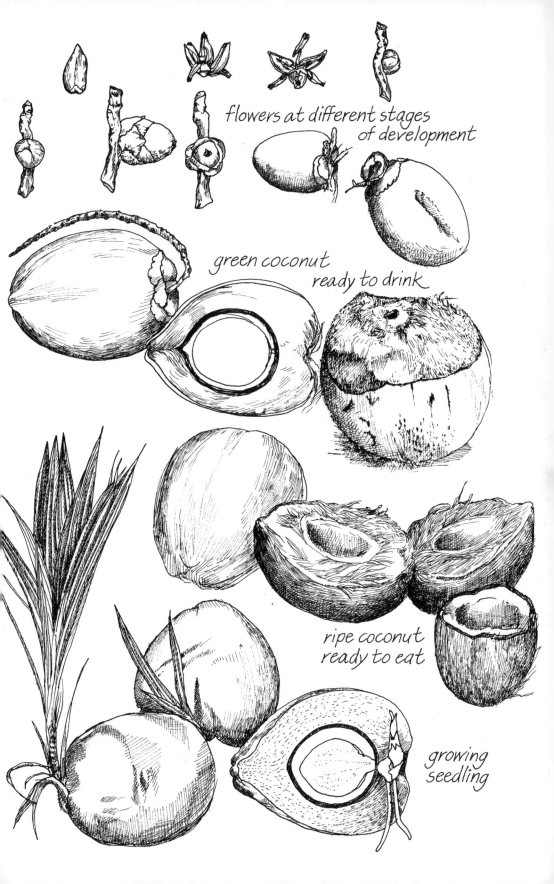

flowers at different stages of development

green coconut ready to drink

ripe coconut ready to eat

growing seedling

The nuts are big and heavy, a foot to a foot and a half in length, about half that thick, weighing about three pounds. The nut contains a single tiny seed kernel beneath one of the three dark spots on the inner shell. The white meat nourishes the kernel as it begins to grow, and the water inside the coconut supplies the moisture it needs. Eventually the kernel sprouts, working its way through one of the soft spots of the hard, woody shell and out through the mass of protective fibers and the husk.

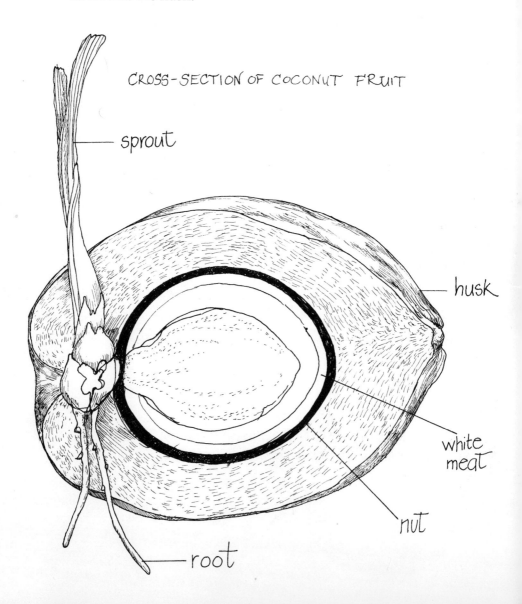

CROSS-SECTION OF COCONUT FRUIT

sprout

husk

white meat

nut

root

You can try to grow a coconut tree from "seed" yourself. You need a fresh coconut with the husk still on it; the coconuts sold in grocery stores and supermarkets have had that outer husk removed. (You can order a whole coconut from Ted W. Miller, The Tourist Trap, Box 291, Lawai, Kauai, Hawaii 96765, for $2.95, including postage. Allow three to four weeks for delivery.)

When the coconut arrives, soak it in water for a couple of days. Then find a pot just deep enough to hold the nut. Put a few large stones or pieces of broken pottery in the bottom of the pot, and cover them with two inches of light, sandy soil. Set the coconut in the pot, bud end up. Pour soil around the coconut until it is half buried. Water the coconut every day, pouring lukewarm water right on the husk.

Keep the pot on a radiator or in some other warm place to make it sprout faster, but make sure that it doesn't dry out. In four or five months, or perhaps even a few months longer, the first narrow green spears will appear. All this time the tiny plant has been getting nourishment from the white meat inside the nut, but eventually, in about a year, it will send out fleshy white roots.

After the roots appear, transplant the coconut to a container about eighteen inches wide by eighteen inches deep. The plant may live for two or three years and grow four or five feet tall, if conditions are right, but don't expect it to bear coconuts.

The warm, damp conditions needed to get a coconut to sprout in your home are a little like those in the tropics, where coconuts flourish with considerably less trouble. From twenty-five degrees north of the equator to twenty-five degrees south of it, in a belt that encircles the earth, are thousands of islands and many more thousands of miles of low seashores. Throughout this belt the sun shines steadily with no cold spells, and there is plenty of water. In our hemisphere these conditions extend as far north as Hawaii and the southern part of Florida.

There are different theories about where the coconut palm originated. Botanists believe that it may have first grown in Malaya or Indonesia. But they do not agree on how it reached so many other parts of the world. One theory holds that the big, buoyant nuts literally floated around the world, carried by ocean currents for thousands of miles, and washed up on low-lying coastal plains, where they took root, grew, thrived, and multiplied. But another more prevalent theory is that coconuts were carried not by water but by man, as he traveled and explored all parts of the tropics.

Although coconuts can grow wild, most of them do not.

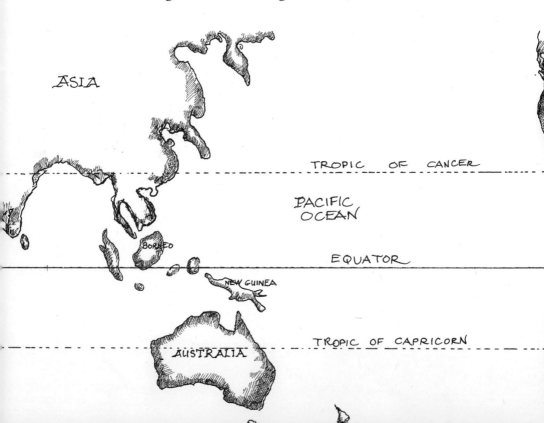

ASIA

TROPIC OF CANCER

PACIFIC OCEAN

BORNEO

EQUATOR

NEW GUINEA

TROPIC OF CAPRICORN

AUSTRALIA

They have been cultivated for thousands of years by people who can support their families with only a few trees. Today most coconut trees are grown on plantations. These plantations may consist of a few dozen trees owned by a small farmer, a few hundred trees producing for a large landowner, or a few hundred acres thick with palms.

In the islands of the Caribbean and along the coasts of Africa and South America, most of the coconuts are consumed where they are grown. But in the Far East the export of coconut products is a thriving business. There the large-scale cultivation with a high yield of nuts per acre is carried out mostly in Indonesia, Malaya, India, Sri Lanka (formerly Ceylon), and the Philippines. The nuts are a principal source of income to areas that must import most of their goods. Coconuts are also a basic food in these places, sometimes the only food to survive a natural disaster, such as a typhoon, which wipes out rice paddies and cornfields.

Virtually all of the coconuts and coconut products imported to the United States come from the Philippines, which was a possession of the United States from the end of the Spanish-American War in 1898 until independence was granted in 1946. Close ties have remained.

Harvesting coconuts is the backbone of the Philippines' agricultural economy. Of the approximately eleven million

acres of coconut palms scattered around the world, four and a half million acres are in the Philippines, a group of more than seven thousand islands with a total land area of 115,600 square miles. Most plantations have less than a dozen acres each. The islands have wide valleys and dense forests, rich volcanic soil, and a hot, humid climate—the perfect place to grow coconuts as well as other food crops.

Coconut palms must be fertilized for maximum production. Commercial fertilizer is one way to do so, but in some places intercropping is a cheap and effective alternative. Bananas, for instance, can be planted among the coconut palms. As each banana plant bears its fruit, it dies off and is left to disintegrate and return most of its nutrients to the soil.

There are a number of different kinds of coconuts grown for their different qualities. One variety, for example, may have the highest oil content, another the highest sugar content. Growers are experimenting with dwarf varieties that are less picturesque perhaps, but are easier to harvest, begin to bear earlier than other varieties, and are also less likely to be knocked down by typhoons. (Remember that a small farmer who loses his few trees in a tropical storm must wait eight years for the new trees he plants to start bearing.)

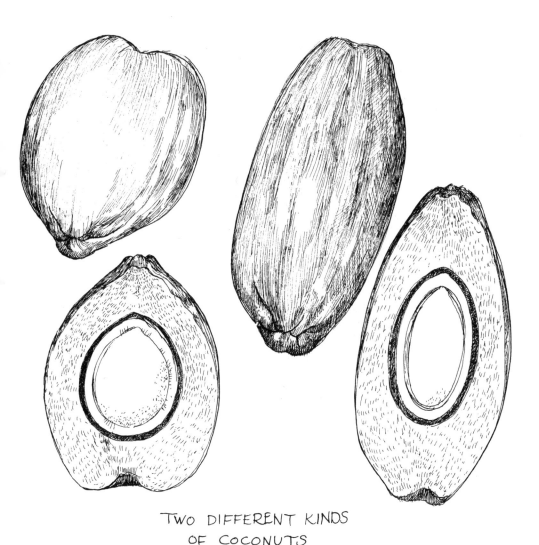

TWO DIFFERENT KINDS
OF COCONUTS

It has also been discovered that the dwarf coconut palm is not susceptible to lethal yellowing, a disease that has destroyed thousands of trees in Florida and on several islands of the Caribbean. Despite its lack of value as an agricultural crop to the people of Florida, the swaying coconut palm is a symbol of balmy weather to shivering tourists from colder parts of the country, and many Floridians are urging that the dead trees be replaced with the dwarf variety, which are less spectacular but hardier symbols of the warm tropics.

DWARF COCONUT
PALM

One problem that cannot be solved by planting the dwarf variety is damage from rats. In some places gnawing rats destroy nearly half the annual yield of coconuts. Metal bands placed around the trunks prevent the rodents from scrambling up the trees from the ground, but they do not deter the colonies already established in the treetops, where generations of rats are born, reproduce, and die, without ever touching the earth.

There are three ways to get ripe coconuts down from the trees. In some places, an agile boy or young man climbs the tree as easily as though he were climbing a ladder. With his long, flat-bladed knife—known in various parts of the world as a machete, bolo, or cutlass—he cuts down the ripe nuts, ignoring the sway of the tree and the long distance to earth. The nuts hit the ground with a sound like the boom of a distant cannon. In other places, the worker ties his knife to the end of a very long pole. The pole sways, the tree sways, and the worker needs a sure eye and a strong arm to cut down only the ripe nuts without bringing down any green ones or damaging any flower buds. The "lazy man's way" is also considered by some coconut buyers to be the best: wait until the ripe nuts fall, and then collect them. This method assures the buyer

that an overzealous picker has not brought down some not-quite-ripe nuts that weigh heavy when he sells them to the buyers but are not ready for use.

However they are gotten, before the ripe nuts travel very far, the thick, fibrous outer husk is removed. Each nut is jammed against a sharp blade—a plowshare, for instance—stuck upright in the ground. After a few stabs against the blade, the husk falls away. The hard-shelled nuts are collected

and taken to buyers. In the West Indies, the nuts are collected in huge sacks and "headed"—balanced on top of the head, an excellent way to carry very heavy weights to their destination. In the Philippines, a farmer usually guides a cart drawn by the family's carabao, or water buffalo.

But some of the coconuts are taken home and prepared in a variety of dishes. In all the countries where coconuts are raised for export and for local consumption, coconut is an important part of the diet once the nut has been opened. Most people who eat a lot of coconut are quite adept with their long knives, skillfully splitting open the nut with a single whack. But for those of us who are not so handy with huge knives, other methods are better and safer.

The three dark brown spots at one end of the coconut are rather soft. Punch holes through two of these spots with whatever sharp-pointed tool you have at hand: an ice pick, or a hammer and a large nail work well. Make sure you pierce all the way through the white meat inside the nut; wiggle the pick or nail to enlarge the hole through the meat. Drain out the coconut water. It has little use; it is not the real "milk" of the coconut that is used in cooking.

Turn on the oven to about 350 degrees, and put the coconut in the hot oven for about twenty minutes. Tap it all over. Then break it open with a few sharp blows of a hammer, or drop it on a hard floor until the shell cracks. As the result of heating it, the brown-skinned meat should separate easily from the hard shell. Use a vegetable peeler to remove that brown skin. You will then have the waxy white meat of the coconut.

In the tropics, where coconut is eaten nearly every day in some form, the coconut is used in two principal ways: it may be grated and added to the other ingredients; or the coconut milk may be squeezed out of the grated coconut, which is then discarded. Sometimes the coconut is used in higher concentrations than at other times. The recipes that follow will indicate how much grated coconut to use and how much water or milk to add to it.

To grate coconut, most cooks in the tropics use a hand grater. The process of rubbing chunks of coconut meat against the rough side of a metal grater, however, is slow and laborious. If you have a blender, you can save yourself a lot of effort. Cut the coconut meat into small pieces, and drop them, a few at a time, into a blender set at high speed. Empty the blender often.

Once the meat has been removed from the nut, it spoils quickly. Keep it tightly covered in the refrigerator for a day or two. It freezes well, either grated or in chunks, and is ready to use almost immediately when you take it out of the freezer.

COCONUT MILK

To make coconut milk, you'll start with grated coconut in a mixing bowl. Pour boiling water or hot milk over it, depending on the recipe, and let it stand for a half hour. Pour the mixture through a strainer into another bowl, using a spoon to press out as much liquid from the coconut as you can. Then proceed with the recipe.

Although many people simply throw away the grated coconut after the milk has been extracted from it, people in the Caribbean use it to make a sweet treat with the interesting name of Love Powder.

LOVE POWDER

Measure the grated coconut left after making coconut milk. Add half that amount of sugar, mixing it in a saucepan. Cook it rapidly for five minutes, stirring constantly. Then cook it slowly for ten minutes more, still stirring, until the coconut becomes golden brown. Eat Love Powder by the pinch, or sprinkle it on pies, cakes, puddings, and ice cream.

COCONUT PUNCH

The water from a green coconut is considered a great treat by people who live in areas where fresh coconuts abound. A thirsty person simply whacks off the top of a green coconut with a heavy knife and drinks right from the nut.

You can approximate that refreshing flavor with ripe coconut by following the directions for coconut milk, using ¼ cup grated coconut and ¾ cup hot water. Let it stand, strain it, and drink.

To make Coconut Punch, add a tablespoon of sugar and chill it well.

Serves 1.

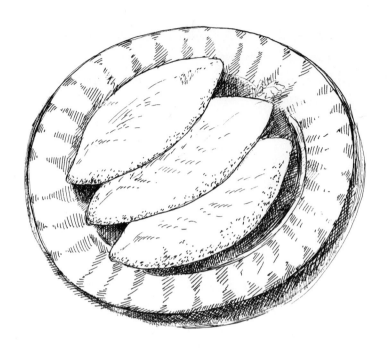

FISH IN COCONUT MILK

    2 cups coconut
    1 cup boiling water
    4 large fish fillets
    salt and pepper

Prepare the coconut milk with the grated coconut and boiling water.

Turn on the oven and let it heat to 325 degrees.

Place the fish fillets in a baking dish, and season them with salt and pepper. Pour the coconut milk over the fish. Bake for about 20 minutes, until the fish flakes easily when you test it with a fork.

Serves 4.

In this recipe from India, the coconut is cooked with the main ingredient.

EGGS WITH COCONUT

3 tablespoons butter
2 tablespoons finely chopped onion
¼ cup coconut
3 eggs
3 tablespoons milk
salt
chili powder

Melt the butter in a small frying pan. Cook the onion until it looks glassy. Add the coconut.

In a small mixing bowl, beat the eggs lightly with the milk and seasonings. Pour the eggs into the pan and scramble.

Serves 2.

Curries are popular ways to prepare rice, meat, fish, and eggs in India and the Orient and in certain islands of the Caribbean. Curry is not one spice but a combination of spices, such as turmeric, clove, cumin, ginger, pepper, coriander, and caraway. In the United States, curry powder can be purchased already blended.

Grated coconut belongs with curries just as ketchup is necessary to a hamburger, and a hot dog is not worthy of the name without mustard or relish. Other condiments such as chopped peanuts, chopped onion, raisins, parsley, and chutney are also served with curries.

In this curry recipe, the coconut is cooked with the meat rather than offered as a condiment.

CURRIED BEEF BALLS WITH STEAMED RICE

1 cup uncooked rice (not instant)
2 cups water
1 teaspoon salt
1 pound ground beef
salt and pepper
1 tablespoon oil
1 medium-sized onion
1 medium-sized tart apple
1 teaspoon curry powder (less if you are not sure that you
    like it)
½ cup water
¼ cup grated coconut
1 tablespoon raisins
1 tablespoon jelly
1 tablespoon lemon juice

Put the rice, water, and salt into a saucepan with a lid. Bring the water to boil over high heat. Then turn the heat to low, and simmer the rice for 15 minutes until all the water is absorbed. (You may substitute your own recipe with instant rice, if you wish.)

Meanwhile, put the beef, salt, and pepper into a mixing bowl. Mix it well and form the beef into balls about the size of walnuts.

Chop the onion into small pieces. Cut the apple in quarters, cut out the core, and cut the quarters into cubes. Leave the skin on.

Heat the oil in a large frying pan. Fry the beef balls quickly, a few at a time, until they are brown all over. Take them out of the pan, and set them aside on a plate. Fry the chopped onion and apple in the pan juices, until the onion looks glassy.

Mix the curry powder with the water and add it to the pan. Add the beef balls again. Cook, stirring occasionally, until the apple cubes are tender. Add the coconut, raisins, jelly, and lemon juice, and cook until everything is heated through. Serve the mixture over the rice.

Serves 4.

Of course, coconut is used in sweet foods in other countries, just as it is in the United States. In Hawaii, the traditional *luau,* or feast, often ends with *haupia,* a pudding made with coconut milk thickened with cornstarch and served on philodendron or magnolia leaves.

HAUPIA

  2 cups grated coconut
  2½ cups milk
  ⅓ cup sugar
  3 tablespoons cornstarch
  ¼ teaspoon salt

Scald the milk by heating it slowly in a saucepan until bubbles begin to form around the sides. Don't let it boil. Prepare coconut milk with the grated coconut and hot milk.

Mix the sugar, cornstarch, and salt in a saucepan. Slowly add the coconut milk, stirring it briskly, making sure there are no lumps of cornstarch left unblended. Cook the mixture over medium heat until it boils, and boil it gently for one minute, stirring constantly with a wooden spoon and making sure that you cover every bit of the bottom of the pan as you stir. This mixture scorches quickly if you don't.

Pour it into a serving dish or individual dessert dishes. Or pour it into an 8-inch square baking pan. When it has cooled, chill it in the refrigerator. Cut the pudding in cubes, and serve it on leaves or on more conventional dessert plates.

Serves 4.

In South America and the islands of the Caribbean, coconut milk is used to make a kind of rice pudding.

ARROZ CON COCO (Rice and Coconut)

2 cups grated coconut
2½ cups milk
½ cup uncooked rice (not instant)
½ teaspoon salt
¼ cup sugar
dash cinnamon
dash ginger
¼ cup raisins

Scald the milk by heating it slowly in a saucepan until bubbles begin to form around the sides. Don't let it boil. Prepare coconut milk with the grated coconut and hot milk.

Mix the coconut milk with all the other ingredients in the top half of a double boiler. Put a lid on it, and set it over the bottom half, partly filled with hot water. Cook the mixture over boiling water for about one hour, stirring it once in a while, until the rice is just tender. Do not overcook it. Serve it warm, sprinkled with more cinnamon or with toasted coconut.

Serves 6.

Here is one of the simplest of coconut candies, popular in the Caribbean.

COCONUT SUGAR CANDY

Measure grated coconut into a saucepan and add an equal amount of sugar. Mix in one teaspoon of water for each cup of sugar. Cook the mixture over medium heat, stirring it constantly, until the mixture is very thick and pulls away from the sides of the pan. Don't let it start to turn brown. Drop by the spoonful onto a sheet of waxed paper.

Number of candies depends on amount of coconut used.

COPRA

ANIMAL FODDER

OIL

PLUS FATS AND ALKALAI →

NEW

POW!

SOAPS

Many Uses, Many Recipes

The Indonesians have a saying, "There are as many uses for the coconut as there are days in the year." The vast number of uses of just the oil alone accounts for most of the days of the Indonesian year, and that is only the beginning.

In those parts of the world where coconuts are grown as a money crop, the most important product of the coconut palm is copra (pronounced KOP-ruh), the dried coconut meat from which the oil is then extracted.

The coconut and the olive are the earliest recorded sources of vegetable oil. In ancient times the coconut meat was ground

65

by mortar and pestle to extract the oil, which was used as a hairdressing and body ointment as well as for cooking. But until a century ago, coconut oil was important only in the Orient and in those areas where coconuts grew. Then a shortage of cooking oils in Europe in the nineteenth century triggered a search for a substitute, and coconut oil became widely used. Today soybean oil is the leading vegetable oil in world production, followed by peanut and cottonseed oil. Coconut

oil trails behind, but its use may spread in the future, because it is cheap and relatively easy to produce.

After the ripe coconuts have been gathered and the thick husks removed, the nuts are opened. The workers squat comfortably, chatting sociably. They hold the nuts in one hand and cut them open with a single blow of their work knives. The coconut water flows around their bare feet; that liquid is the one part of the nut that is wasted.

The opened nuts must be dried promptly. Coconut meat is about half water, and the high concentration of moisture and fat in the nuts causes the meat to turn rancid quickly. Contamination by bacteria or mold must also be avoided. Drying prevents both.

The most efficient drying method is by forced hot air, but it involves equipment that is much more expensive than most copra growers can afford. Only a change from many small farmers to a few large growers is likely to increase the amount of such equipment in use. The more usual method is kiln drying. A smoldering fire of coconut husks is built on the floor of the stone drying hut, the split nuts are placed on the grate above the fire, and the hut is closed up. In a day or so the nuts are dry, the meat turned a grayish color. The cured coconut meat, the copra, is easily separated from the shell and bagged for shipping. Kiln drying is cheap and fast, but it sometimes results in scorched or burned copra.

In some places the copra is sun dried rather than kiln dried. This method is simple and inexpensive and yields good white copra—if it doesn't rain. But it rains often in the tropics, and even when it does not, the humidity is usually high. If the copra doesn't turn rancid before the sun has time to dry it, it may be ruined by mold.

In the Philippines, and in other countries that export copra, the moisture content must be reduced to about 20 percent by some drying method before the copra leaves the farm. Then the copra is delivered to the warehouses of firms that buy and ship it to the United States and other countries for refining. The drying continues in the warehouses, called "bodegas" in the Philippines, until the moisture content drops still more. It continues even after the copra is spread out on the decks of ships for the voyage across the Pacific. By the time the copra reaches the United States, the moisture content is down to 3.5 percent.

Prices paid to coconut farmers are based partly on moisture content; the buyer does not want to pay for water, and he also does not want the copra to spoil in transit. On certain islands of the West Indies, where the farmers deliver the copra directly to a small refinery, each sack of copra is checked with an instrument that registers moisture content. Copra with moisture content over 7 percent is rejected.

Although most people in coconut-growing areas now buy factory-processed oil, for many years families made their own. If you want to try making a little raw coconut oil, here is how to do it:

Follow the recipe for coconut milk on page 54, using 2 coconuts and ½ cup of hot water. When the mixture is cool enough to handle, knead it with your hands for 5 minutes. Then strain it, pressing the grated coconut, a little at a time, against the side of the strainer with a wooden spoon to extract as much milk as you can. Boil the coconut milk gently for an hour or so to evaporate the water and leave the oil behind. Watch it carefully toward the end to make sure you don't burn the oil.

Although most copra is exported for refining to industrialized countries like the United States, the copra-producing countries like the Philippines are expanding their own refining facilities, in order to keep a larger share of the profits at home.

The first step in the commercial process of making coconut oil is to crush and grind the dried copra and then to press the oil from it. The oil content of copra ranges from 50 to 70 percent, depending on the method of drying. (Soybeans yield only about 17 percent oil.) Ten coconuts produce about five pounds of copra, which in turn yields about one quart of oil. Some refineries cook the ground copra first in order to

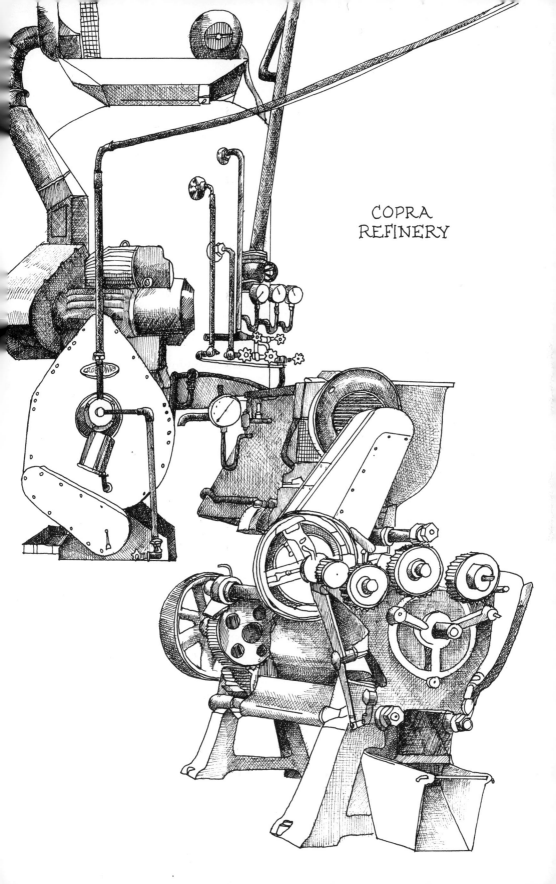

COPRA
REFINERY

extract the oil more easily; some big refineries also use solvents, or a combination of the two methods, for maximum yield.

The reddish-brown residue left after the oil has been extracted is called "coco meal" or "coco cake." It makes good animal food, high in protein, and is used locally and for export.

Next the raw oil is neutralized. At this point the oil is dark and full of impurities, and the smell of coconut is strong. Ingredients added to the oil combine with the impurities to form heavy particles that can be separated out when the oil is pumped through a series of filters.

After filtering, the oil is clean but still smelly. Several hours of boiling eliminates that odor. A second filtering yields oil that is colorless, odorless, and tasteless. But since completely colorless vegetable oil is not very appetizing, the refiner who wants to sell the oil to home cooks must now add food coloring to restore the attractive golden color.

One of the principal uses for vegetable oils in the United States is in making margarine, but so far coconut oil has not proved suitable. Margarine was first developed in the 1860's. Napoleon the Third of France sponsored a contest to find a substitute for butter, and the contest was won by Hippolyte Mège-Mouries, a chemist who figured out how to convert vegetable oil into a spreadable substance. One of the problems of coconut oil, however, is its narrow "plastic range," the temperature at which margarine is soft and spreadable. Butter stays plastic, somewhere between a stiff solid and a liquid, over a wide temperature range. But coconut oil goes quickly from a liquid at room temperature to a brittle solid when it is cooled. A chemical process called "hydrogenation" changes this quality in many oils, altering the molecules so that they are plastic over a wider range of temperatures. But coconut oil is not affected by hydrogenation, and processors who want to use coconut oil in margarine have to combine it with other oils.

There is a second drawback to coconut oil. All fats and oils are made up of both saturated and unsaturated fats. Some medical experts believe that saturated fats build up a fatty residue in the arteries of the body, gradually blocking them and causing damage to the heart. Although there is no conclusive evidence that saturated fats are directly responsible for heart ailments, many people believe that they are and avoid eating them. Animal fats such as butter and bacon are known to contain many saturated fats; most vegetable oils consist largely of unsaturated fats and are, therefore, thought to be more healthful. Coconut oil is an exception; it is high in saturated fats.

An American doctor interested in the nutritional value of coconut oil says there is no evidence that people in coconut-producing and coconut-eating areas have more heart ailments than anyone else; in fact, his studies show that they may have fewer. But manufacturers and consumers are afraid to take the chance.

Another use of coconut oil is in filled milk. In the process of commercial butter making, the butterfat is entirely removed, leaving a thin, bluish by-product with the same food value as skim milk. The taste and nutrition can be restored to this by-product by replacing the butterfat with coconut oil. Although only about 2 percent of all the milk sold in the United States is filled milk, some experts see it as a possible way of feeding the hungry people of the world, utilizing a by-product that is usually fed to animals. The dairy industry opposes filled milk as a milk substitute, just as for many years that industry fought against the competition of margarine as a butter substitute.

Approximately 20 percent of the coconut oil produced in the United States is used in some kind of food, such as desserts and toppings. Food chemists continue to look for more and more ways to use the versatile oil.

Coconut oil has also found its way into many products that have nothing to do with food. One important product is soap.

Like many other common things that we take for granted, soap has a long story that dates from the earliest recorded history. It is usually tied to the history of bathing, and there have been times when neither one was very popular. The ancient Greeks enjoyed taking baths, but they didn't know anything about soap. Instead, they used a tool resembling a shoehorn to scrape the dirt from their bodies. Meanwhile, in another early civilization (one legend credits the Gauls, another the ancient Romans), it was discovered, probably quite by accident, that a sticky mixture of fat and ashes could be combined with water to get the dirt off skin and clothes much better than plain water did.

Soapmaking improved through the centuries. Only the rich

and royal could afford soap, but not all of them took advantage of it. By the eighteenth century, however, housewives in the American colonies were saving animal fats and dripping water through ashes to produce lye. They knew that boiling lye and fat together resulted in soap for some inexplicable reason. And basically that same chemical principle still operates today in the highly efficient production of soap and synthetic detergents.

Coconut oil makes excellent soap, producing a quick, thick lather. Whether soap is made on a small scale near local coconut-oil refineries, or in huge American factories, the process is similar. A combination of fats and oils and an alkali, such as caustic soda, are boiled together until the soap curd rises to the top. With or without further refining, the curd is poured into molds to harden and then cut into bars. Coconut oil is nearly always part of the recipe for shampoos, shaving creams, and other special soaps that need to make a lot of lather.

The cosmetic manufacturers use coconut oil in lipstick, suntan lotion, and other skin creams. Chemical manufacturers use coconut oil in the production of fatty acids and glycerine, a by-product of soapmaking. Drug manufacturers dissolve vitamins and certain medications in coconut oil. The list, already long, continues to grow.

Next in importance to oil and its products is charcoal made from coconut shells. During wartime, coco-shell charcoal was used in gas masks. More recently it has been used for cigarette filters. Coco-shell charcoal is also used in refining liquid food products and in purifying water.

Charcoal is mostly pure carbon, made by partly burning the hard shell of the coconut to drive off all the other chemical substances and leave the carbon behind. Charcoal is used as a filter because of its microscopically pitted surface that catches and holds impurities as gases and liquids pass through it. This process of catching and holding is called "adsorption" (different from the process called "absorption," in which impurities actually soak into and become part of the absorber). Coco-shell charcoal is naturally highly adsorptive, and the adsorptive powers can even be increased by a special chemical process.

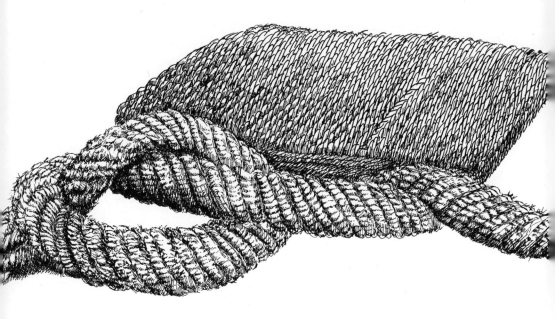

The fibrous husk of the coconut, which takes up about a third of the bulk of the nut, is used to make the fiber called "coir" (pronounced to sound like *coil*). When the fibers are soaked in salt water, they become soft enough to spin into rope or twine or weave into mats. Products made from coir are extremely durable and are more resistant than other fibers, such as hemp, to the effects of salt water. Most coir manufacturers are located in India and Sri Lanka. Not much coir is imported into the United States, which uses rope and twine made primarily of hemp.

Coir dust, another product of the husk, is used in coconut-growing areas for making fertilizer, timber, plastic-board insulating material, and dozens of other industrial products.

Many more products of the coconut palm are used locally and seldom find their way into the world market. For instance, the leaves of the coconut palm are woven into draperies, fans, brooms, chairs, baskets, hats, and even roof thatches. The burlaplike covering at the base of the palm leaf can be made into slippers and sun helmets. The roots yield medicine and dyes. The water in a fresh green coconut is a favorite drink in the tropics. Free of impurities and containing the equivalent of two tablespoons of sugar, coconut water has also been used as an emergency substitute for glucose. During World War II doctors and medics dripped it directly into the veins of wounded soldiers when no sterile glucose solution was available.

The sap of the coconut palm can be collected by binding together a clump of flowers and bruising the tip—yielding up to a gallon a day of the sweet, cloudy, brown juice with no coconut taste. If allowed to ferment, the sap produces a drink called "toddy." It is also distilled to make vinegar and boiled down to make syrup and sugar. And once the old tree is no longer producing nuts, the trunk can be sawed into a beautiful hardwood, called porcupine wood.

People who are involved in growing, processing, shipping, and selling coconuts are constantly searching for new ways to use the products of the coconut. People who enjoy the taste of coconut are always looking for interesting new ways to eat it, too. After you have sampled all the old favorites and have investigated some unfamiliar cuisines from other countries, try simply adding coconut to other basic recipes.

For instance, use coconut in traditional Waldorf Salad, the creation of a headwaiter of the famous New York hotel. His recipe called for apples and celery mixed with mayonnaise. Later someone else added chopped walnuts. Here is the newest version, invented especially for this book.

COCONUT WALDORF SALAD

1 big red apple
1 large rib of celery
mayonnaise
½ cup coconut
lettuce leaves

Wash and dry the apple, celery, and lettuce leaves.

Cut the apple into quarters, remove the core, and cut the unpeeled apple into cubes. Cut the celery into small pieces. Mix the apple and celery, and add enough mayonnaise to hold the pieces together.

Arrange lettuce leaves on two salad plates, and put half the salad on each bed of lettuce. Sprinkle coconut over the salad.

Serves 2.

Although sweet potatoes (dry and yellow) and yams (moist and orange) are not related, both grow mostly in the South and are often used interchangeably in old Southern recipes. Both taste so good with coconut you'll wonder why you never tried the combination before.

COCONUT SWEET-POTATO CASSEROLE

4 large sweet potatoes or yams
½ teaspoon salt
2 tablespoons butter
2 tablespoons brown sugar
4 tablespoons coconut

Wash the sweet potatoes or yams and boil them unpeeled in salted water for about 30 minutes, until they feel tender when you test them with a fork or the point of a knife.

When they are cool enough to handle, peel off the skins (they slip off easily). Mash the potatoes with a fork in a mixing bowl and stir in ½ teaspoon of salt.

Turn on the oven and let it heat to 350 degrees. Lightly grease a 1½-quart casserole with butter or margarine. Pile the mashed sweet potato into the casserole and smooth the top.

Melt the butter in a small saucepan, and stir in the brown sugar and coconut. Spread the mixture over the top of the sweet potatoes. Bake for 15 minutes.

Serves 4.

Fried chicken is one of America's favorite foods, and each part of the country seems to have its own version. Try it with a coconut coating, and let the oven do the frying. You'll please fried-chicken lovers in every state.

COCONUT CHICKEN FRY

4 chicken legs and thighs (or other parts)
½ cup flour
1 teaspoon salt
¼ teaspoon pepper
1 egg
1 tablespoon water
½ to ¾ cup coconut
¼ cup butter or margarine
1 tablespoon vegetable oil

Wash the chicken parts and dry them with paper towels.

Put the flour, salt, and pepper in a small paper bag. Put one or two pieces of chicken at a time into the bag, hold the top closed, and shake the bag to coat each piece lightly.

Scramble the egg and the water in a soup plate or pie pan. Spread some of the coconut on a plate or piece of waxed paper. Dip each piece of chicken into the egg mixture, and then roll it in the coconut. Put the coated pieces in the refrigerator for about 1 hour so that the coating will set and not fall off when you begin to cook.

Turn on the oven and let it heat to 400 degrees. While the oven is heating, put the butter or margarine and the oil into a baking dish or a large, heavy frying pan and set it in the oven. When the butter or margarine is melted and bubbly (about 10 minutes), carefully remove the hot pan from the oven and set it on a cold burner or on a heat-proof pad.

Arrange the pieces of chicken, skin side down, in a single layer in the pan. Bake for 30 minutes. Take them out of the oven again, and, using a pair of tongs or a fork, turn over each piece. Put the pan back in the oven, and bake for 30 minutes more.

Serves 4.

Gingerbread dates back to ancient times and the discovery of spices, and it has been a favorite in America since Colonial days. It can be served in a variety of ways. Here is one, traditionally flavored but including coconut and topped with a coconut glaze.

COCONUT GINGERBREAD

½ cup water
½ cup butter or margarine
½ cup sugar
½ cup molasses
2 eggs
1½ cups flour
½ teaspoon salt
1 teaspoon baking soda
½ teaspoon cinnamon
½ teaspoon ginger
½ teaspoon allspice
½ cup (or more) coconut

Turn on the oven and let it heat to 325 degrees. Grease an 8-inch-square cake pan.

Put the water and butter or margarine into a small saucepan, and heat until the butter is just melted. Pour into a mixing bowl, and add the sugar and molasses. Beat in the eggs.

In a separate mixing bowl, put the flour, salt, soda, spices, and coconut. Mix them with a fork. Add these dry ingredients to the first mixture, and beat until thoroughly blended.

Pour the batter into the cake pan. Bake for 35 minutes, or until a toothpick stuck into the center of the gingerbread comes out clean. Frost it in the pan with Coconut Glaze. Cut in squares and serve it warm.

Makes 9 squares.

COCONUT GLAZE

⅓ cup butter or margarine
⅔ cup brown sugar
3 tablespoons milk
½ to 1 cup coconut

Melt the butter or margarine in a saucepan, and stir in the sugar, milk, and coconut. Spread the mixture on a warm cake, and put it about 4 inches below a hot broiler for 3 or 4 minutes, watching carefully so that it does not scorch. (Wear oven mitts to protect your hands.)

COCONUT-PINEAPPLE GINGERBREAD

Follow the recipe for Coconut Gingerbread, *except:*
Use pineapple juice in place of the water.

COCONUT-HONEY GINGERBREAD

Follow the recipe for Coconut Gingerbread, *except:*
Use honey in place of the molasses.

Try making everybody's favorite breakfast treat with coconut.

COCONUT PANCAKES

1½ cups flour
½ teaspoon salt
1½ teaspoons baking powder
¼ cup coconut
1 egg
1¼ cups milk
1 tablespoon vegetable oil

Heat a griddle or large frying pan while you are mixing the ingredients.

Put the flour, salt, baking powder, and coconut in a mixing bowl, and mix them lightly with a fork.

Add the egg, milk, and vegetable oil, and beat until the mixture is smooth.

Use a paper towel with a dab of butter or margarine to grease the griddle. Sprinkle a few drops of water on the griddle; if the drops dance before they sizzle away, the griddle is hot enough. Pour the batter in pools with a large spoon or small ladle. When the pancakes are bubbly in the middle, flip them over with a pancake turner. Cook for another few seconds, until they are brown when you lift up an edge.

Serve with syrup, or spread with butter and sprinkle with toasted coconut.

Makes about 16 pancakes.

COCONUT DESSERT PANCAKES

Follow the recipe for Coconut Pancakes. Then mix one 7-ounce can of crushed pineapple and its syrup with $\frac{1}{4}$ cup of brown sugar in a small saucepan. Bring to a boil. Serve over the pancakes, and sprinkle with toasted coconut.

An old Scottish recipe gets a new taste with coconut.

COCONUT SHORTBREAD

1 cup butter or margarine
½ cup sugar
2 cups flour
1 cup coconut

Put the sugar and butter or margarine in a mixing bowl, and blend with your hands (if the butter is cold and hard) or with a wooden spoon until they are thoroughly mixed.

Add the flour and coconut and work them in, making a stiff dough. Shape the dough into a ball, and chill it in the refrigerator for a half hour to make the dough easier to roll out.

Turn on the oven and let it heat to 300 degrees.

Dust a rolling pin and a table or counter top very lightly with flour. Pat and roll out the dough until it is a little less than ½ inch thick. Use a knife or cookie cutter to make small cookies. They can be set close together on the ungreased cookie sheet, because they do not spread. Bake for 10 minutes. The cookies will not turn brown. Use a spatula to lift the baked cookies onto a wire rack to cool.

Makes about 2 dozen small cookies.

These Coconut Brownies are made with brown sugar and have a butterscotch flavor. You can also add coconut to a standard recipe for chocolate brownies, using 1 cup of coconut instead of the nuts.

COCONUT BROWNIES

1 cup brown sugar
¼ cup butter or margarine
¾ cup flour
1 teaspoon baking powder
½ teaspoon salt
1 cup coconut
1 egg
1 teaspoon vanilla

Turn on the oven and let it heat to 350 degrees. Grease an 8-inch-square cake pan or a 9-inch pie pan.

Put the brown sugar in a mixing bowl. Melt the butter or margarine in a small saucepan, and pour it over the sugar. Mix well. Let it cool while you are preparing the other ingredients.

In another mixing bowl, measure the flour, baking powder, salt, and coconut. Stir them lightly with a fork.

Add an egg to the butter-sugar mixture and beat it in well. Stir in the vanilla. Add the dry ingredients and mix them thoroughly. Spread the mixture in the pan. Bake for 20 minutes. To test for doneness, press your finger into the top of the brownies. If your finger leaves only a slight dent, the brownies are finished. If they are still soft, bake for 5 more minutes.

Put the pan on a rack, and let it cool for about 20 minutes. Then cut the brownies into squares.

Makes 16 brownies.

These recipes are just a beginning. Coconut seems to crop up everywhere. As you come to enjoy the versatility of the coconut, you will appreciate the Indonesians' belief, "as many uses as there are days in the year." With the advances of technology and the ingenuity of curious cooks, that may soon prove to be an understatement.

Index
denotes illustration

93

95